Songs of a Chicken Bone

Godspower Oboido

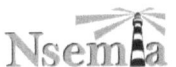

Copyright © March 2014

All rights reserved.

This publication may not be reproduced, in whole or in part, by any means including photocopying or any information storage or retrieval system, without the specific and prior written permission of the author and publisher.

This book is sold subject to the condition that it shall not, by way of trade or otherwise, be re-sold, hired out, or otherwise circulated without the author's or publisher's prior consent in any form of binding or cover other than that in which it is published and without a similar condition including this condition being imposed on the subsequent purchaser.

First Edition: March 2014
Published by Nsemia Inc. Publishers (www.nsemia.com); Oakville, Ontario, Canada

Edited By: Charles Phebih-Agyekum
Cover photograph: Baek Koeun
Author phtograph: Sughoon Jung
Cover Design & Concept: Godpower Oboido
Cover Layout: Danielle Pitt
Layout Design: Kemunto Matunda

Note for Librarians:
A cataloguing record for this book is available From Library and Archives Canada.

ISBN: 978-1-926906-34-8

for
Esther and Samson Oboido,
Friends, teachers, parents
of blessed memory

TABLE OF CONTENTS

ABOUT THE AUTHOR - v
FOREWORD - vii

JOURNEYS AND ADVENTURES

The morning of birth - 3
Song of the forest - 4
It begins - 4
Home coming - 5
Home Coming II - 7
Flight - 8

PLACES AND PEOPLE

For those that are missed - 11
A Redemption Song - 12
City girl - 13
Little Girl - 13
The Village Girl of Mzimba - 15
A Poem - 16
The underground - 17
To the soothsayer - 18
Not My Friend I - 19
Not My Friend II - 20
A tale of two cities - 21

NIGERIA

Beasts of this nation - 27
This maddening soil - 28
The fisherman and his son - 28
They lift up holy hands - 29
Kwashiorkor - 30
No place like home - 30
Prison of peoples - 31
We must choose paths 32
Justice - 33

THOUGHTS AND OBSERVATIONS

Romeo and Julian - 37
Rainbow, water, fire - 37
There are no dreams in times of war - 38
That child is long gone - 39
The atheist's God - 40
Musings - 41
Entanglement - 41
Silent Night - 42
Pensive - 43

AFRICA

We have come a long way - 47
I am African - 48
Poetry for the iroko men - 49
Africa Is Not My Country - 50
Apartheid Boys - 51
Stranger - 52
Sons of Africa - 53

MISCELLANEOUS

If you must pronounce my name - 57
Remembrance - 57
Poetry - 58
To a young Nigerian poet - 58
I am my father's child - 59
Seduction - 59
Insomnia - 60
Slum Dwellers - 60
Three strangers - 61
Path of rain - 62
Exchange with a Hummingbird - 63
I sing of summer - 64
Come my darling - 65

ABOUT THE AUTHOR

Godpower Oboido is an exciting new voice in the African literary scene. He is a poet at the Stables Theatre, in Hastings UK, with style greatly influenced by classical literature as much as it is by the buzz of modern society. He was a finalist in the 2010 Future of Nigeria Awards, where he was among the 100 of the best and brightest Nigerians under thirty. Godpower Oboido's works have been published in The Istanbul Review, Saraba Magazine, African Write, and Nathaniel Turner, among many others.

FOREWORD

Poetry is the highest achievement of English literature, and it is so little valued in the modern world that we are in danger of neglecting the fire that keeps the forge of language going. Currently, the most commonly celebrated poetry in English is the rhyming derived from the Jamaican tradition, which promised so much when it was first heard in Britain. Since then, the most exciting voice I have heard is African.

I count among my friends people from The West Indies, Ghana and Nigeria. In January 2009 the first annual meeting was held of The Stables Poets, at the theatre of that name in Hastings UK. We have since been greatly entertained by people of different countries reading poetry in English, mostly their own work. When Godspower Oboido first read to us I heard the voice of Africa. He has been blessed with wide experience and with the grace to be true to his roots.

The iroko tree has shaded all that Godspower has done, and in Benin, where the poet grew up, the people there will say he has been blessed by Ajani, goddess of the sands, who inhabits the iroko and to whom pregnant women pray for a quick and happy birth. Iroko has brought its blessings in the lives of English children, too, since it was for many years the preferred timber for the seats of 'bobby's hat' roundabouts in the playground.

Come to Oboido's work and you will enjoy sharing the resonance of his voice and his joy of poetry.

Peter Harvey, Hastings
December 2012

# JOURNEYS AND ADVENTURES

The morning of birth

On one early harmattan morning
Began my journey here,
Through paths unknown
When the stream of passage broke.
Sister was out playing.
Mother pushed- but I wasn't coming out.
Time silently drifted by in the other world
Where many children rode on unicorns
Or waited next in line to be born.
They watched me stuck in transition,
In the morning of birth.
They finally bade me goodbye
And then I was born, at night.
I was cupped in mother's palm.
Lifting me up, her new born, she smiled and said:
"It must have been by God's power".
But I ignored all this, I was a stranger
Here in this intricate world.
Eyes shut in fear; uncertain of this chosen path,
I burst out with my earth-welcome cry
That attracted women to the room,
My sister now admiring me from a corner.
The women cut the umbilical cord,
But that was not a separation.
No brilliant fireworks, but singing and clapping
Welcomed my joyful arrival here
As the women danced around me, a new born.

Song of the forest

I embark on a fishing trip with my friend
In the tropical forest of the Delta.
The streams –Liquid songs
Of enchantment –ran true.
Young boys, we were
Seeking fun and adventure
In a forest that bowed in silent fear
Reeking of initiation.

Deeper in the forest, we heard
The beautiful birds of paradise,
The conversation of sheltering tall trees,
The sounds of nude bamboos
As lazy branches simply flirted in the wind.

It begins

With goodbyes that paw the air,
With tears that flood memory's lane.
It begins,
The journey over thousands of miles
With jumping trains and catching planes
But destiny is a plume
That I, a bird of passage must flutter through.
Was not my umbilical cut
That I may roam in pursuant of a dream?
Tell mother then, you robed messengers
That I set forth at dawn
When I take on metal wings
Let her bid goodbye from atop

For I shall call through the golden rays of dawn,
Piercing through rebellious clouds.
I shall taunt the earth, flat beneath me
Like the belly of a placid lake
And say "you have no hold on me"

It begins,
Like a tale, this journey begins.
Let it be told, lest it dies in the throat.
See, I anticipate it like gathering storms.
If what must be must be then let it be.
Let this story be told. Let it be.

It begins,
The journey of the prodigal.
This labyrinth amazes me sometimes
But I am a bird of passage
And my life is a journey, always a journey.
I do not call lands my home, yet.
A passer through, I am a tourist of life.

Home coming

It hasn't been long that I've been away
But I return home today,
My tongue unturned but my accent changed.

The girls I meet are ill-mannered,
They stare at me and push Blackberry buttons.
"Where do you come from?"
One of them asks, she winks.
"Your voice is sweet and I like it"
They do not know me.

The boys spot dreadlocks and wear their trousers low,
Mimicking the Hip-hop stars they have seen on TV.
I act somewhat strange, or so people say,
I talk less and I stare more at the charm of nothingness
Through the dust-speckled glass of green cabs.

Too hot the eye of Heaven shines on me,
But to be unclothed is to be mistaken for a mad man.
I am not one, but there are many around; madmen,
Beggars, they crowd street corners and market squares,
United in unbargained fate.

They drink from the sewer and sleep on dirt heaps.
Elsewhere the high and mighty, frocked up in agbadas*
Eat fat chickens and dine on green pastures.
Rapture! I call and pray for it.
My nation is plunged into insanity.

Agbada - a flowing wide sleeved robe worn by men in much of West Africa

Home Coming II

Who will tell them that I have come home
From the lingering lane in a daze,
Now that the village town crier I used to know
Has become Minister of Information?

Announce my unsavoury appearance,
Tell them I have come
With some of the white man's ways
But I have not betrayed the black man's brain.
I have come home to bring the war of the world.

"I hear the troublemaker is back."
It is me they talk about, you see.

I have come to lick the bottom of the stew pot
(Mother had said it tasted better)
And curse its blackened buttock afterwards.
I have come to seek out my oppressors
And bite their fingers pointing at me.

The boiling water with its great tribulation
Will test the patience of the pot.

I have sauntered home, the wind my guide,
With a swagger of rediscovery
To remake my past and correct my future.

I have come home, a prodigal,
But I have not come to beg forgiveness,
Rather, to ask more of my inheritance.
The homecoming shadows my departure.

Flight
Abuja to London

Seatbelt fastened,
Glistering morning sun Peeps
Through my porthole sheepishly –
With the familiarity of parting
As I begin to pluck these lines
From the lips of the prodigal wind
Plotting a coup with the placid clouds.
I pluck these fertile lines
From the nonchalance of time
As it passes and listens to the melody of silence.

The distance gently conquered.
The clouds, ever obedient in their position
Cast shadowed spells on the Libyan Desert.
The passengers are soon united in sleep
Awaiting the flight's end; I join in at intervals,
With afro-beat music dominating my ears.
No longer do I enjoy the silent anthem of the clouds
Hidden outside my window blind.

Flying into Europe, the earth is salted by snow.
Soon I am greeted by England,
By those green fields carpeting its landscapes.
I realise that I have been away too long.
I give a familiar smile of greeting.
The glory of the football stadiums
Rises on my wings in splendour.
London beckons me; the familiar smells
From her street corners, the fashion and coffee shops;
I return to the land of frequent tea and coffee
That never rebels against faithful consumption,
To London's frequent drizzle
That never morphs into courageous rain.

PLACES AND PEOPLE

For those that are missed

Who hugged me
And kissed my cheek.
Remembering the times
When we ate meat and potatoes,
The times of laughter
Over meals in Cedar room,

Times of glorious fellowship
In Great hall.
We sat around the fountain
And talked about our futures,

Of reuniting again,
How I long for it now.
We played football on the lawn.
"Easy, easy" I would scream at the girls.

We walked around the woods and lake,
Holding hands, smiling and talking,
Birds singing for us.

At departure our tears fell
On the lichened patio.
We took our separate paths,
Many oceans apart to dawn lit vistas.
Do these memories haunt you I wonder
–Or is it just me?

I miss you, here again as always
In the stillness of this autumnal wind
Blowing in my face,
Bringing the memories once again.

A Redemption Song
for Bukola Elemide, Asa

The hunter now learns to pluck his wisdom
From the blabbing of this child's *ijala* –
From the voice once calling at the fringe,
That has now given wings to the wind.
The bird of peace, known to have come
From alien lands passes above my head
And transport your dreams
Above the heights of New York and Osaka.

Out of the forest of bamboos singing lazy noon songs
Has emerged the roar of the iroko tree,
From the chirping of the flock of manic forest birds
Has emerged the lullaby of the lady song bird.
The *hawk* has landed to prey on us,
Negligent ones who have become repentant children
Of your pungent message; you haunt us in lyrics.

You are the queen of the hallowed strings
Whom mother Africa sings of in many voices
As the music itself that did not die
In the solitary street of the thrush throat,
But escaped to wake a slumbering world.

Your songs make us dream of change
For the hopeless little stars of Makoko[1]
Whose dreams are resurrected from the slum.
They too now dream of becoming superstars
When with many lights across life's stage
They will bow not to the clapping audience,
But to you, whose life has become their redemption song.

---

1 A slum area in Lagos, Nigeria

City girl

She wears western clothes:
    Scarves, long pants and nice tops,
Walking around London in a svelte figure.
    The city girl, a young baobab,
Looks like a girl I know, like a girl from my country.
See how she rolls those big bright eyes,
    Pregnant like a West African full moon.
Look at her afro hair, blown up
Like a fruitful mango tree.
    Look at her strong back
    And long black arms.
The city girl is no city girl at all -
She looks like a girl from my village,
Like the dancing girl from my mother's tales.

Little girl
Beatrix Wynn, with love

Yesterday when I bent over
And reached out to touch you,
Your eyes twinkled
With butterflies and fireflies
That sang of a bright future.

Seeing you
I learned
That the best things in life
Are little, in charmed frames,
Like you, little girl.

Your feet were charming,
Running in the corridors,
Broadcasting news of the
New teddy bear.
Seeing you,
I learned to live
In a world like yours,
Without fear
Of what May brings
Or of April's frequent showers.

Was it not you, child,
That I watched,
In open admiration
Each time I walked pass?
Feasting gazes, exchanging
Greetings with you, little girl.

In your charm, so tenderly sweet
Little child, I am reminded
Of how the peace of heaven
Kisses the stillness of the sea,
And how the fishes
Swim in blissful freedom.
Yesterday now dances
In the valley of the past,
But you left happy thoughts
Morphing in this heart of mine
That remembers you, Beatrix Wynn.

The Village Girl of Mzimba
Rhoda Martin

She clutches a child on her back
That sags like a sturdy tuber of yam,
Striking an image of motherhood.
She strides gracefully on the dust
Carpeted streets of Mzimba.

Some villagers along the path
Feast their prying eyes on her.
They know she is not from Mzimba,
But they love her like one of theirs.

The young boys, holding their thumbs up,
Have learnt how to say "what's up?"
They must practice it with her some day
In exchange for a foreign accent.

The sun caresses her alabaster skin,
But her smile is un-tanned still
As she walks on Mzimba's streets.
The white Somerset girl has become
The new villager of Mzimba.

Songs of a Chicken Bone

A Poem

For Kseniya Doronina

Her face peers from the corner of the mall
Where our eyes first meet and tweet.
She smiles radiantly. A Russian girl.
I had heard many stories of them.
We hug; then a civil kiss on the cheek.
Her blonde hair drops like waterfall on her shoulders,
Firm and boastful of her sweet youth.

One evening at mine, over a cup of Earl Grey,
A university apartment in old Saratov,
The sixth floor, room number thirty seven –
I am somewhat James Bond.
She demands to take her tea with lemon – a very
Russian girl.
I toss my gaze at her fluorite crystal eyes
That no fitting metaphor can describe

How they dazzle
Like stainless goblets from ancient Rome,
Like spring water of the lost Atlantis.
I laugh, she smiles, and we chat
Listening to Roo Panes, a troubadour.
My face becomes laughter's playground
But my gaze still keenly stamped on her face.

She speaks, softly, of spring's bloom
And a walk in the main city park
But there is something she does not understand
That fairer than spring's lotus blossom
Are the daffodils in her pungent smile
In unison singing, a silent hallelujah.
More enchanting are the lakes of passion in her eyes
Than the great waters of River Volga.

I speak of beauty, quite frankly as a poet,
Of what it means to be beautiful
And I tell her beauty is not in the eyes of the beholder
But it is in her eyes, cat-like and meek in the dark.
I speak repeatedly of her ethereal beauty
But I lament that this poem
Lacks the words to describe it.

The underground

It flares in an instant, this city
And its brightest things swing about the place.
But underneath are displaced ghosts.
We, commuters all, take their place

To Edgware Road and Marylebone,
To Piccadilly, to Westminster and West Finchley,
Oxford Circus and Regent's Park.
Underneath is a vibrant city,

A webbed universe
Of British ingenuity.

Immigrants in transit to work,
Models crossing long legs
Minding their business
Like they mind the platform gaps.

Beggars, some of them refined,
Smile and watch you walk by,
So you exchange your coins
For a moment's tripping chords.

The city is connected,
Above and underneath.
But this city is tormented they say,
When we frenetic ones go to rest.

To the soothsayer
I will not consult you.
But tell me,
Will poets lie?
And will politicians
Break their promises?

I will not consult you,
But you tell me,
What must be
December's fate
In the harmattan?

Tell me about yam and oil,
About their romantic fate
In the mouths of the famished,
Or about the unfortunate antelope,
Will it end up in the hunter's belly?

Will Jonah be swallowed
By the giant whale,
Or will he swallow the whale?
Cast your lot now and speak,
Soothsayer, will you?

I will not consult you,
But you must tell me soothsayer,
Of your own future.
What will become of you?
Will poets lie?

And will politicians
Break their promises?
Will the fortune teller
Himself, someday grow rich?
Cast your lot now and say.

Not My Friend I

When I hear the dialect of his gun,
That terrifying laughter of the crick-crack,
I am reminded that he is not my friend.
He who scratches my head against the wall
In a bullying permitted by his uniform,
And watches my blood trace its way to earth.
How can he say that he is my friend?

He advertises on yellow placards
Hanging behind him, 'Police is your friend'
Yet he hates me like an enemy.
I know he is not my friend.
But I wonder what makes us different.
Why our friendship was bound to fail.
I should have known when he cuffed Rotimi's wrists,
When he fettered Enabulele's feet,
That he was not our friend.

One day he called me
And said that he was still my friend,
But only when I give him twenty naira[2]
Should friendship ever be bought?

---

2 *Nigerian currency.*

Not My Friend II

Then yesterday he stopped me at Oregun
With a whisper of mischief,
His eyes had calculated what I would be worth.
"Where are you coming from?" he asked
From those lips, black as his uniform.
"I'm waiting for a friend from Ibadan,"
I answered politely, I tried.
"Where are you heading to, GENTLE MAN?"
He didn't really think I was gentle,
He just liked my nice clothes and PUMA shoes.
"To the British embassy," I said.
"Now you must identify yourself,"
"Haba!" I exclaimed. "This is my fatherland,
Can't I walk around freely?" I protested.
"THIS IS STOP AND SEARCH MY FRIEND"
I opened my wallet reluctantly,
The photograph of a white girl flashing in his face,
"Who is she, the girl in the passport?" he asked.
"A friend in England," I answered.
"Your girlfriend, she is your girlfriend."
I knew that was coming. He smiled
As he said that. I said not a word.
He knew what I thought of him then –an idiot.
"Identity, I want proper identity,"
He barked as a colleague of his showed up.
I brought out my international passport.
They grabbed it along with my travel papers.
Without looking at them they screamed
"Fake! Fake! These documents are fake!"
I hadn't seen such mad men in ages.
My passport and documents were flung
Back at me, I was told to run away.
A hard nut to crack –I was–so they thought.

But a new catch was in the offing for them,
Another gentleman –judging by his appearance.
He was dragged to the corner of a black van.
"Pay money, pay money – or I'll slap you now,
I'll shoot you now," He was shouted at as I moved on.
Thinking of my friend as he called himself,
A disgrace to the nation he serves in uniform.

A tale of two cities

Lagos

The myriad yellow coloured *molues*[3],
Are like swarms of metal bees transporting a throng of
Energetic Lagosians from rush hour bus stops
Where LASTMA[4] officials await traffic offenders,
To different locations with thriving parties;
Women flaunting brightly coloured damask *igeles*[5],
Tokens of their feminine liberation and fashion.
Talking drum beats chatter with spirits of dancing foots,
So elephantine stomping the soil of Lagos.

Passengers, transporters, hawkers, commuters
And political campaigners go about their daily business
Buoyed by the city's 'do or die' spirit of competition;
Area boys and area fathers, positioned at sharp
Street corners plot and wait for unsuspecting victims.

In Lagos, the invisible undergrounds, panti and kirikiri[6]
Are cesspits of the city's hardened notorious criminals
Where incessant cries stab the air –some begging, others curse:
"God punish all our thief-thief politicians wey put us here."

---
3 *What Lagos commercial mini-buses are called*
4 *Lagos State traffic management agency*
5 *A piece of head tie clothing worn on the head by many women in Africa*
6 *Panti, Kirikiri: prisons in Lagos*

The sermon of a trousered preacher, wiping his sweat
Of hardship, as he bends over an ill-tempered conductor
Comes assured: "God go save Nigeria, Him go give us safe journey."
The chorused "Amen" response from the passengers
Competes with the molue driver's deafening juju music.

A white photographic journalist jostles for space
And captures a panoramic view of the metropolis
In flash seconds; glossy magazines smile in anticipation.

The crushed lips of the suffering many and the grinning
Frame of the smiling few; political supporters all
Chant in patriotic unison 'EKO O NI BAJE O'

London
The grim faces of London's many immigrants
Tell a thousand untold tales: the homeland forgotten,
The promise of a better future now gone rotten, the bills
That cast a heavy burden on their shoulders.

The liquid song of River Thames is an orchestra
For passing lovers, holding hands, smiling and talking;
'The Spirit of Chartwell' once an enticing fantasy.

Ahead the romance is different,
Uniformed teenagers wear striped blue socks,
Whisper tender kisses to mates; their unsaid goodbyes
Billow in the wind before they join their calling mothers
Waiting on the front terrace of East London flats.

A click captures London in a tourist lens: two Scottish pipers,
Big Ben, The Houses of Parliament, Buckingham Palace...

In Liverpool Street an Italian restaurant, the hub of travellers,
The destitute and homeless, plates hot meals at night.
"It's a Jamie Oliver recipe," the chef assures them with a smile,
Himself buying British manners. London sells it right.
London Bridge is falling down in my presence, still falling down,
But only in songs and rhymes; London is ever undying.
A bustling lifestyle frocked up by exotic young men and women:
The London eye, in stealthy coyness captures only the seen;
But the spirit of London is the unseen.

NIGERIA

Beasts of this nation

I will not look to the distance
In search of those who castrate my dreams,
Certainly not down at this path I trod
In search of those who castrate your dreams,
Our dreams that were yoked in one embryo.

You cannot say you aren't devoured.
I see those premature pains in your wide eyes.
Your once blossoming smile has been deflowered,
Mine is just a caricature.
You know we have the plague spoken of.

They liken our fate to that of those
Whom vultures laugh and wait for,
Whose visible chest bones have been numbered.
Now they gleefully long for us to drop dead.
You know we are tormented.

I must purge my native womb
In search of those who castrate my dreams,
Our dreams, buried in greed
By the marshals of corruption.

This maddening soil

A wanderer I traverse
On this soil, still green.
Where I feel a foreigner.
My mind travels too fast,
First betraying me,
But I return a wanderer still
To find erosion here:
Sand of my childhood washed ashore,
The whirlwind swept away our fair goods,
Ravens poked our skulls.
What else have we here?

The fisherman and his son

Father
My child, night and day I've toiled,
Nothing could I bring forth,
Not a single fish, child.

Son
The fishes swam ashore
When they heard your song.
You are no friend of theirs.

Father
Night and day I've toiled,
Nothing could I bring forth,
Not a single fish, child.
The fishes are all dead
(Whispers)
From the poison of oil
Spilled on our waters
By foreign oil companies.
But *Argungun** forever excels.

Son
What will my hungry belly eat?

Father
Our hungry bellies, my child.

*Argungun –a popular fishing festival in Northern Nigeria

They lift up holy hands

Behind the pews of God
Hide those that make a war at night
And pray for peace at day's dawn,
Pretending to put out the fires they started
So the multitudes can cling to them.

They lift up holy hands,
Reaching for God in mockery.
As the priest recites his litany
And sprinkles Holy water
That cleanses not blood-stained
Hands, those holy hands lifted up,
Reaching for God!

Kwashiorkor[7]

He has tiny legs and a swollen stomach
Like a yearlong pregnant woman
Guilty of sacrilege
And cursed never to deliver.
He is but deprived and malnourished.

Your legs are also tiny.
You were thin only a few years back,
But now, on your corrupt seat of politics
Your pot-belly is no longer concealed,
Resembling only a fattened toad.

Your shape is round,
Because you use tax payer's money
To drink pepper-soup and Gulder beer.
Like the child you have left bmalnourished
You suffer from kwashiorkor.

*Kwashiokor: *Is a form of malnutrition that occurs when there is not enough protein in the diet.*

No place like home

Today I received news from home,
Another bomb blast rocked the city
Of Abuja. I am not untouched by it.
When I hear you say that there is no place
Like home, I'm like "Oh yeah, I really think so, too"

---

[7] *A form of malnutrition that occurs when there is not enough protein in the diet.*

Sometimes when I am no longer homesick
It is because there are many at home, sick.
When I am no longer homesick, you see,
It is because the government is still very sick.
When I say I am no longer homesick,
I mean just that.

One day mama travelled home to the village
And she never returned. It happened at home.
Sixteen people on a bus to the land of no return.
Home is not always the distance across,
It is the simple things treasured.
Where the treasure is, there the heart will be also,
And where the heart is, there home will be also.

Prison of peoples

I echo Fela's pungent message
For the first and the repeated time
Of the cesspit, that marketplace of many scoundrels
Where water, murky with Shell spillage now has an enemy.
Scaly skirted mamiwatas* swim off in crowded rivulets.

The unbridled madness of our incarcerated society
Has overwhelmed us like mother's love, undying,
In this revolution of chaos-thick demo-crazy
Where military boys only became morons in agbada.

Army man carry him trouble with yanga**
Go 'mamaput' shop. "No serve me sour soup"
He pre-warns. I do not know where to place him –
Military boy or democratic moron.

Then he opens sporadic fire on civilians.
"Bloody civilians"
The suffering and the smiling are imprisoned
In this common man's 'big oga sah' mentality.
I break free, rebel of no nation.

*Mamiwaters: *Mermaids, venerated by some in West, Central, Southern Africa and the African Diaspora in Caribbean, North and South America.*
**Yanga: *Show off*

We must choose paths

Here brothers, at this cross-road
We must choose paths. Together we may fall,
Parted, we will stand, I promise.

We must choose paths now, as you
Blow the horn for your emancipation
With many bombs and machetes.

We must root out our umbilical cord,
Crush that which binds us
Now that Canaan is swamped
With blood and honey.

Britain will not stop being Great, I promise,
If this area be no longer Niger,
If river Benue's tributary turns on its course.

Justice

Obobaifo was well beaten up.
Bloodshot eyes, swollen face.
Odigie was thrown into prison.
And Enofe was shot dead,
Buried the following day by the police.
Little was the bribe he refused to pay.
They said he was a robber, like the others
There were witnesses.
Kadiri was one. Emokpae was another.
Lasisi was the third;
But remember that all three are policemen.
When justice is thus served,
What words have we?

THOUGHTS AND OBSERVATIONS

Romeo and Julian

There could not be a story of more woe
Than that of Julian and Romeo.
This once ribald tragedy
Has completely gone wrong with gay delight.
The entire world is a stage,
But we players became frivolous
And betrayed the cue whispered by morality.

"Kill Juliet, kill Juliet
Who needs her here?
Two men can play this even better,"
The audience screamed with immoral certitude.
Ah! Wonder of wonders.
Sodom and Gomorrah had just been rebuilt
In this animalistic play of the new generation.

Rainbow, water, fire

Rainbow, water, fire.
I see a rainbow bending over in your backyard,
Warning the flood's raging courage.
I see you smiling and saying,
"God is good and His word is true."
You rejoice in His covenant birthed anew.
Revenging floods will not consume our world again,
But the rainbow one day will go,
I wonder if you will still rejoice in God's covenant
When the heavens in a great voice pass away
And the elements with fervent heat melt away?
Revenging floods will not consume our world again.

Rainbow, *water*, fire.
I hear you talk about water every day,
You talk about it heating up our world.
I do not hear your words and here begin to fret.
Revenging floods will not consume our world again.

Rainbow, water, *fire*.
I hear you talk about global warming,
How you warn that it could change our world.
This could end our world.
Too hot the belly of the earth has become.
I hear you talk about global warming
That it could be the final instrument of destruction.
It could be the final instrument of destruction

There are no dreams in times of war

When galloping elephants are chased
By butterflies coloured in blood,
It is a nightmare you must awake from.
When sugarcanes lose their sweetness
It is because they were planted in bloodied soils.
Swans will neglect the lakes
And frogs will occupy them like a plague.
When the moon no longer shines,
It is because the earth sees your tears.
When the sun forgets its season, winter has its day.
Dreams in times of war become surreal nightmares.

How do you dare to dream
When your eyes are ambushed by fear
Under a naked roof, metal fireflies hovering above,
Carrying the sting of death in priority mail?
You gaze down at the child in your arms,

His legs and arms chopped off. Do you dream
That he'll still become a doctor one day?
What is a dream without a sleep?
Tell me who dreams in times of war,
Who dare shut their eyes and go to bed?

Can you dare to dream that your little girls
Will spend their future with the boys
They grew up with on the red soil of childhood,
Now taken as child soldiers to war,
Devoid of the memories of innocence?
Do you still dream?
How many wars must we suffer in a lifetime?
What will be the children's fate
Growing up in the battlefield of a broken home?
Tell me who dreams in times of war.

A child long gone

They have reprinted the image again
Of the little African child.
Yes, the same who was in TIME magazine
And comes up in Google searches.

Chest bare and begging to be fed,
His nostrils hosting wild flies,
His eyes unleavened and sunken.

He has no shoes on his feet,
He cannot even stand,

His young body is old and frail,
On the point of collapse.

His mama is just a hag,
Chest bare and also begging to be fed.

Welling tears gather round your eyes
As you stare at the mother and her child in pity,

But every now and then
It is the same picture of this child in this pitiable state
That is used for every campaign when he is long gone.
Or tell me, when will he ever die?

The atheist's God

Many say in their hearts there is no God.
In their lips are doctrines of atheism
But in their hearts,
Some knowledge of God
Or a yearning for one.

There was a certain atheist
Who swore there was no God
Until a certain day
When his shop was on fire,
Called to the scene he cried
"Oh my god!" I ask therefore,
Atheist, what God have you?

Musings

Tide and market come and go, I know,
But why did my mother travel and never returned?
Or why did father sleep and never woke up?
Why are children born to die?
Why do some die before they are born?

Tell me why your tears repel my smile,
Why the world is so big that it separates us,
Why you live at one end and I live at the other,
Why it is so dark here, yet elsewhere it is day;
Is the cloud at war with itself?
...
Hush my darling and listen
To the timid laughter of the wind,
To the impotent music of life's rustic flute.
Wait, and watch in the uncertain labyrinths of our world.
Wait, wait until these musings corrupt your laughter,
Until time and chance bargain on our behalf.

Entanglement

Life is a repeating cycle, a nascent entanglement.
The agama lizard boasts at the embassy of the crocodile,
But soon its head that once capered with conceit
Is chopped off in submission.

Who can be born a man without a woman?
Or who can be born a woman without a man?
Life is a repeating cycle, but do not brag woman,
Do not say "I beget the man" or he will puff up

And remind you that you are drawn from his ribs.
Life is like tie and dye, you cannot withdraw
The colour from the fabric once it is dyed.

The sun must dominate the day
But the moon must watch the night
When the stars will be sky's brilliant children.
Life is a repeating cycle, criss-cross hatch of sorts.

Silent Night

On a still night, heaven my shelter, I stand amazed
At the peace of the uncounted stars.

Under the dangling parables of moonlight
Is the dance of the wind
To the distant melodies of a silent orchestra.
The dark clouds gossip silently
As they saunter through the sky veranda.

Heaven yawns and pour its libation
On the head of my mother's child.
I pause in admiration of this night,

This silent night, when the angels are still
And the rustling of the trees
Brings in the calm.

I remember the little children
When they would gather for the tales
Of their ancestors and the cunning tortoise,
Of diverse mythical gods colonizing the galaxies.
A silent night of peace and charm.

Silent night: Babies will be born
And men will depart this world asleep.
When the shadows of human silence unite
Our dreams are a gurgling night drama
That wreathes our unconscious minds.

Pensive

I am awake early in the morning.
My prayers do not rise
To the summit of Hermon, I regret.
I am caught up
In something bigger than me, again.
My face is the shallow dance
Of the eastern masquerade.
The smile on my face died yesterday
At birth of the morrow.

I am travelling again,
To and fro into the past and future,
On the familiar labyrinth
Where Yesterday twins today.
I fear they will marry tomorrow.

I am travelling
The solemn backyard
Of many thoughts about nation,
The green hills
Of unanswered questions
And flat carpet
Of questions unasked.
I am bespectacled
In my bewildered gaze
By distant frustrations and worry,
Over how long we will remain

Betrothed to this maddening state,
But one day perhaps
The sun will learn to shine
Again. I know I need faith
If I must get up and walk,
But I have been made a chief,

Entitled to sit on this chair,
Spruced up in this pensive mood
And ask forlorn questions
As do the other compatriots.

AFRICA

We have come a long way

Does it never bother you, my brother,
That time has eaten up our past,
That the miles we conquered are now vanquished?

We can no longer trace our way back.
For Ignoble idiots were our fathers,
Not the husbands of our mothers;

But those clad in military frocks
And flamboyant agbadas
Those tyrants and dictators,
On whom the hope once glimmered.

But who have now
Led us through this path
Of many wars, death and suffering.

We have lost friends and families along the way.
How mad we became I do not know.
We have come this far and lost it all, or nearly all.

We have come a long way,
But what is there to show for it?
The miles completed now exact revenge
As we travelled to this place unknown,
Through the rugged path now elastic.

I am African

Tame and bind me
And I shall emerge
Like the Zulu warrior.

Bind me up,
I shall flourish like the antelope.

I'll roar like the lion
And explore like the giraffe.

I am he that never dies,
My spirit lingers at the shore.

I am the city
Set on Mount Kilimanjaro
Under tropical African sun,
I cannot be hidden.

I am he that has plucked wisdom
From the teeth of the moon
That inspires our nightly tales,
Tales of my brave ancestors,
Of the kings of the skies.

My ego is fed
By the beat of the warrior's drum.

I am he that never cried
Under the bestial whips of your ancestors.
I am what I am. I am African.
This Afri*can,* yes I can.

Poetry for the iroko men

I invented a simple vision
Of the mosquito feasting
On the bud of the hibiscus
Sucking its sweetening nectar
Promising never to be drunk
Again on our blood-red wine

I invented a simple vision:
The king of the jungle appointed
The tortoise as poet laureate.
Ah, *Ojualangba*[8] was brilliant,
Birds were lulled to sleep,
Little chicks gathered
By their mother for her fowl tales;
Brilliant in true rendition.

I invented a vision
Of the merchant of the Libyan Desert
No longer lusting over American Rice
No longer crushing the Arab flowers
Unspoiled in their youthful bloom.

I invented a vision
Of the pregnant Ugandan mosquito
Dancing at a feast of nectar
With all her invisible children

I invent a lucid vision
Of the iroko men, assembled
In a poetic commonwealth
Dialoguing for Africa's change.

---

8 *The face of the lizard*

Africa Is Not My Country

I am not a common idea in the foreign man's head.
Not his senseless nigger
Fighting another frivolous serial war.
I am not from a line of HIV infested whores,
I am not the child with the swollen stomach
With flies humming around his eyes.

I am not the foreigner's African.
No, I am not from his naked Africa,
Not from that ditch of savages
Awaiting his benevolent redemption.
I am not the African in the foreigner's head,
Not from the Africa
That he thinks dances in his pocket of loose change.

See how they talk of Africa with disdain
As if we are cursed to be what we are.
They talk of the primitive,
But civilization was drawn from Africa's breast,
From the founding clay of Egypt.

They talk of Africa
As my grandmother's village, only a patch,
Devoid of intelligence and culture.
Let them write their own stories as we write ours.

They talk of Africa as a place unlived-in,
Except by people on one day safaris
Who die the next day of poverty.

They often talk of Africa as a place
Lost in a jungle, in the middle of nowhere,
Where domineering monkeys traverse
The trees in a survival-of-the-fittest show.

They speak of Africa as my country,
Not a continent, second only to Asia in size.

I am no true African, they say,
Because I cannot speak Swahili.
"That's what my friends in Kenya speak
–so you should, you're African, right?"
Yes, right!

Apartheid Boys

I hate to think that you have copied the colonial man's ways.
Remember how cruel he was to you back in those days?
Now you don his coat and smoke his crack pipe.
Woe to you brother, sired of this colour of my skin,
For your brutal betrayal of brotherhood,
That you betray the sweat of the struggle to free Madiba's land,
That you must now slap my face like the white man of yesterday.

Stranger

Today I long for her sweetness,
Her reincarnated prodigal call now
For I am joined to her
In eternal matrimony.

Progenitor of all people,
She smiles to me with her spirit.
I am not separated from her.
My umbilical is buried in her soil
Where I must be laid to rest.

Today I long for her wise folk tales,
Her pristine culture,
Her people, her history.

How can I sing her song here
Where I am only a stranger?
Where I weep when I remember her land,
The dance of her daughters.
I long for her sweetness again.
Her reincarnated prodigal call now.

Sons of Africa

Someday the sons of Africa will emerge
From behind the wall of Kilimanjaro.
Some day they will sail home
On the waters of the Zambezi river.
Some day we will return home –not from afar off.

Someday when the sons of Africa , you and I,
Will till our richly blessed land,
Our proud sweat feeding the earth.
It's the simple things we will enjoy
 –Yams roasted in backyard plantations,
Dipped in palm oil and eaten with pride.

Someday the sons of Africa
With unfailing strength will till our soil,
Not searching for gold and oil
To be sold to the foreigner for a shekel.

Someday,
We'll watch village boys swim with the hippos
On tranquil waters that run truly with mirth.

Someday the sons of Africa will return
Not to the future, but to our past
When we gathered on moonlit nights
And enjoyed the brilliant folk tales
Of our brave ancestors and the cunning tortoise-
The simple things that we once enjoyed.
Someday, someday,
We'll watch our boys sit outside their huts again
Learning proverbs and philosophy from the egg-head,
And then the moon will smile on them again.

I sing of the coming day
When the sons of Africa will be boys forever
Ungrown in the politics of our fathers.
I write again of moonlit nights, our visions
Shining brighter than the night eye of heaven,
And we'll play 'tom-tom-tom' on the goat skin.
The little boys will cut sticks to make night fires,
No longer will they wield the evil fire sticks
Eternally searing the innocence of their childhood.
Some day when the sons of Africa
Will return home,
The simple things will be our joy:
Our past, our innocence, our pride, our culture,
ourselves –
We, the sons of Africa.

MISCELLANEOUS

If you must pronounce my name

You must correct your sibilance
And instruct your tongue.
Like a woman in labour
You must push, with effort
To twist your tongue like mine,
Then try, try again.
You must circumcise your tongue
If you would pronounce my name.

Do not corrupt my name
With the blandness of your tongue.
My name is my destiny,
The belief of my people
And the eternal truth of life
Did you not know that?
If you must pronounce my name
Then reassemble your vowels and syllables.

Remembrance

Dry waters fall from my scaly eyes,
And run down on these pebbled cheeks.
Grief perfumes the air
And leaves it grasping for breath.
Decade is buried in time
But mother has still not returned.
Lost are we, her children, in this cavern of loss
Where pain has no memory.
Death's sting no longer claws it wings.
My ears now hearken only
To the throat of silence
Howling in the corridors of yesterday.

Poetry

Is the dance of pretty African girls
Impressing their men in evening shows,
It is in their long tripping steps.

Is the musings of Olaudah Equiano,
The ballads of slaves sold across the Atlantic.

Poetry is in the African songs of enchantment.
Is the town crier's craft,
His succinct announcement scouting for ears,

The harmonious beat of the talking drum,
The fisherman's solemn invocations.

Is the chilling landscape of Winter,
The unforgettable memories of Summer,
The fresh inspiration of Spring
And the comedy of autumn's uncertainty.

Poetry is the music of the soul,
The romantic enchantment of the mind.

To a young Nigerian poet

Now that our writers have become
Priests to *Ifa*, they all spot dreadlocks.
I, a loner not a poet, laugh out loud
For I am not enticed by their
Pretty poems of nothingness.
The shallow lines, like the Ifa priest's
Prosaic incantations, do not entice me.
But you, young poet, must know
That the prophet is a messenger

But not a courier man,
That writers are like messengers
And not celebrities.
Let a spade be called a spade.

I am my father's child

I am
My father's child.
Was tender and beloved
In my mother's sight.

"You must bury
Your head, child,
In your books,"
He would frown
And say,
I still remember.

"You must become
Something in life,
Anything child,
But not a policeman."
I am my father's child.

Seduction
Her eyes were pregnant
Like a cursed full moon
Speaking of things apparent.
She sat next to me
In the nameless barber's shop
And brewed an evil plan.
"You are not as innocent as you claim,"
She said lecherously, ready to devour me.

Our friends left the shop,
Left me alone with the devil's girl.
Her fiery passion unbridled,
She flipped over on me
Like a possessed masquerade
Flaunting her frontals
Till I could break free of her spell.

Insomnia

The unholy children of the night
Have come for your daily bread,
Ravening restlessly
Like scavengers at your window.
The life left in you is a wandering ghost.
You stay on watch all night long.
You hear the crack of the caller's gun
And prepare to meet your God
In spirit and in truth.
Your sleep is broken and tormented.
You've been made an insomniac.

Slum Dwellers

You mustn't promise the pig
A decent home on the mown lawn,
Never try to entice it
With the smell of freshly cut grass.

Do not beguile gentle larks
With music among ravens,
Do not promise limbs to the serpent,
That it should walk again.

Earth's dusty smell has become
The serpent's sweet potash,
Though mother earth loves to rock
The serpent's plain belly,
Teasing and taunting it daily
With stories of former limb glory.
Earth is the serpent's home still,
Its fate and destiny.

Never threaten the homeless
With rumours of insecurity,
With promise of urban development.
A slum for thugs and the destitute
They will fondly call home.

Three strangers

Snowflakes drift gently down
In neglect of a passing night,
And memories of a fading day.
No neighbours wish 'goodnight'
They are all gone
To fly white kites and hunt for fireflies
In the playground of the moon
With stars at their fingertips.

I look out of my window
And see three strangers
Resting from their journey.
My watching eyes, heavy with sleep,
Plead to retire to bed in the hope
Of flying white kites and hunting for fireflies
In enchanted dream lands.

My sleep a direct flight to dawn,
No white kites nor fireflies.
Then I look out of my window.
The three strangers sit still
On the old lichened bench.
I jump out of bed, my blanket I throw
In pity to cover their cold feet
"You must cover yourself sirs.
Where do you come from?"
I'd learned manners for strangers.
But they do not say a word, not a word,
Neither do they break their gaze.
Then, as if as the breeze blows,
I know who they are and whence they come.

Path of Rain

Celestial dialogue, loud and raging
Call through the grey sunset.
Dark clouds
Swaddling the belly of heaven
Enjoy a lazy ritual dance.
Lightning travels through
Scattering furrows in the sky
Like neon colonies of Seoul.

In a sudden burst of anger
Rain drops on sprawling wilderness,
On desolate wastelands, kissing
Darling buds of tender herbs
Causing them to spring forth anew.

Exchange with a Hummingbird

1

The hunter's son has learned to plucks words
From the lips of time and exchange them
In the market of conversation.
He says to the Hummingbird perching on the tree:
"Hummingbird, I want to be free just like you,
To spread my wings and fly away
In realms alien to the world's way.
But I am human ensnared in a body cage
And what is my fate?"

The hummingbird sings him a song:

2

What can make you content, child of sorrow?
Tell me, child of sorrow if you know
How it feels to be above, free but lonely.
Skyline's outcast, always wandering coldly!
Up here I'm a wanderer under the sky.
When through grey clouds I fly,
My life is not a beautiful poem
Not a colourful rainbow in Heaven's realm.
Unsheltered, the rain touches me first
So does the sun, the snow, the fog and the frost.
Sometimes I want to be free too,
Along with the host of the sky, plentiful.
To perch on soils, to walk and search for food!
But tourists and hunters, like a surging troop,
Scare us, so we find contentment in the sky!
You will find yours on land, son of a hunter, if you try.

I sing of summer

Summer is gone and winter's here
Where the anticipation of a dry, sunny day
Is drowned in the wetness of England.

Here on this old country lane
Where flower stalks are gravely despondent
By winter's frequent drops of rain.

The buds grieve their bruised ego
And bend their heads in shame.
Oh England, you are wet.

Today I sing of summer, of sun rays,
Bright and rekindled, imprisoning this English gloom,
Of kids flying rainbow-coloured kites,

Their sand castles touched
By the visiting tide –coming and going.
I sing of a carnival of laughter

Of summer's market of fun.
I sing of the summit of Hermon melting,
Of grasses lying low with broken pride
Tickled by the smile of the sun

And in familiar fondness, rising to play.
I sing of Heaven holding its peace for once,
Of rain seeds retracting to the clouds,
The orphaned wind wandering the four corners.

Come my darling

Your love bade me welcome
When I was uncertain of this path.
You remember how I cried,
How we cried in turn
When I was uncertain of our destiny
But safety was in your loving arms
And solace in your smile.

But come now again to me, my love,
Come to me, my darling,
Sing for me again like you used to,
Teach me your proverbs,
Let me listen to the wisdom from your lips
Or will you tell me stories of Heaven?

I have tried to be a man
Ever since your departure
But in my trying I have realised
That your love was the greatest thing,
The greatest strength of all.
I am helpless without it.

Come back virtuous woman,
Let me boast a thousand times of you,
Come back, mother
Who have given to me my life.
Let me give something back, pray.

-The End-

www.ingramcontent.com/pod-product-compliance
Lightning Source LLC
Chambersburg PA
CBHW030453220526
45464CB00006B/2525